```
>: 458 1285 483 64 85 Heart rate: Optimal
>: ACCESS
>: *** ****
```

> "As I was walking down the stair
> I met a man who wasn't there;
> He wasn't there again today
> Oh, I wish he'd go away."
>
> **HUGHES MEARNS**

Credits

Created and written by Jared A. Sorensen

Illustrated by Manning L. Krull

Layout and design by Daniel Solis

Players and playtesters, past and present:

Topi Makkonen and the Finnish Mystery Agents

Andrew Johnston and the PortCon 2004 Mystery Agents

Tom Bisbee and the BisbeeCon 5 Mystery Agents

The Dartmouth Mystery Agents

Neal Durando and his "Hollow Men"

Alec Fleschner and his Mystery Agents

Mike and **Ramee Gentry**

Jürgen, **John**, **Annie**, **Jason**, **Clinton**, **Brennan**, **Luke**, **Dro'**, **Thor** and all the folks I've played this game with in various convention halls and hotel rooms (I'm sure I forgot some people)

Special thanks to:

Rebecca for putting up with her arachnophobia-suffering game designer husband

Matt Snyder for getting me to write this game in the first place

Devin Townsend for inspiring the title

[redacted]

Dear Jonas,

I hope everything is well with you. Mama and Papa are fine.

I am writing to you a bit early because some interesting things happened today and I wanted you to know about them. I understand how hard it must be for you to be away from us and maybe this will help pass the time.

I woke up before sunrise this morning and could not get back to sleep, no matter how much I tossed and turned. The sky was changing from black to gray when I left the house. It was so early that almost nothing was open save for the newspaper kiosk by Cafe Station.

(I am sure you are laughing hard right now at the image of me waking before dawn!)

Because the weather was pleasant for this time of year and because I felt like doing so I was dressed in a light coat and simple leather shoes. This is not important to the story but I feel compelled to discuss these kinds of details.

On the way to the tram station, I stopped in at the kiosk and bought some tobacco and cinders. As I have said, nothing was open -- not even the cafe -- so I was content to walk to the next stop and help the city to wake up.

Two things happened then (and this is the reason I am writing). The first event was that I noticed something lying in the middle of the sidewalk between the kiosk and the tram stop. At first I thought it to be some kind of strange street sculpture but as I drew closer I understood it to be not a sculpture but a great fish. The smell is what convinced me! Upon closer examination of the thing I saw that it was a large shark... easily as long as I am tall, possibly more.

The shark was incredibly wide, as if it recently enjoyed a gluttonous meal, perhaps foreboding its demise. Its eyes were bright red and surrounded by bloating, wrinkled white skin. Its gills were dry and similarly red. The smell (as I have said) was terrific. I walked around the shark a few times and thought of perhaps buying some paper to sketch it (such was its size and peculiarity) but I soon grew tired of its stench and its bulk and its sheer unusual-ness. I walked on to the station.

The ride was uneventful and I stayed on through Central all the way to Boxer, such is my appreciation for this kind of travel. I think that our auto-trams are among the finest I have ever ridden. Ultimately, this is unimportant and I will get to the second event.

As you know, Boxer has still not totally recovered from the incident and repairs continue, thus I had to get to the street via an alternate route from the normal skyway bridge over the canal. As I walked up the stairs to the street I saw what would become the second unusual thing that I witnessed today: a man, swarthy and mustachioed in the manner of a foreigner. He was seated as a small table (of the type used by street vendors or magicians) and as he was dressed smartly in a tuxedo, I assumed at first that he was one of the latter. Perhaps, on second thought, he was after all.

No matter. The man himself was not terribly unusual. Rather, it was the feat he was undertaking. He sat in a chair at the table with a napkin tucked into his collar the way children and oafish people sometimes do when eating supper. The table was decorated with two candles (lit) in silver candleholders and on the table between them were the parts of a disassembled bicycle. The man (seeming not to even notice my presence) picked up some part of the bicycle and began to eat it.

I was transfixed at the sight of this strange behavior and watched as he finished eating the piece and proceeded to select and consume another. I watched him for about fifteen minutes. Neither of us spoke. I left the scene somewhat shaken and disturbed. I remember seeing a phonograph beside him. It was playing music but I cannot remember the tune.

Viktor and I will be attending the kinetoscope today to watch the animal executions. As I said, Mama and Papa are fine. The city is lonely without you. Have you heard the news? The attacks grow more and more frequent as time goes on. They say that the agents have a purpose above and beyond any kind of participation in the Great Conflict. I wish you were here to explain these things to me.

I look forward to your next letter and even better, when you finally come home. Keep safe and well.

Your brother,

Willem

Willem

You awake to find yourself sitting in a chair in
the middle of a twelve-by-twelve foot white cell.
There is a sleek black desk in front of you.
On the desk is a small black book.

> Get book

You now have the small black book.

> Read book

You read the book.

> Help

I don't know what you mean.

> Please, help me

I'm not sure I can do that.

INTRODUCTION//

BEGIN TRANSMISSION

> “
> This is a game planet.
> **WILLIAM S. BURROUGHS** ”

Lacuna Part I. The Creation of the Mystery and the Girl from Blue City is an experimental roleplaying game...and you're part of the experiment, whether you realize it or not. If you're unfamiliar with the activity of roleplaying, this might not be the best choice for your first game. Then again, I've had people tell me it's the first game they've played. This is the "second attempt" of the Game, as I call it (rather than a "revision" or "second edition"). The first attempt was successful but incomplete. With this second attempt, I hope to repair any damage I may have caused.

Control, represented by the player (or players) running this game, should read the entire book, including the special sections designated as White, Deep Blue and Black. Under no circumstances should anyone except Control read these sections. Failure to cooperate could result in official sanctions from Control and possibly termination with the Company.

The following sections common to many roleplaying games are missing from this one:

// 1 What is a roleplaying game?	// 2 How to play this game
// 3 Example of play	// 4 Sample scenario

If you don't know the answer to the first question, either you should put this book down or have someone in the know explain the activity to you.

The second part is partially covered in the proceeding sections but much of it is left intentionally vague. The last two parts of absent altogether because there is no "example of play" that would suffice in demonstrating how this game works. A "sample scenario" is similarly useless and has been omitted. The best way to play this game is to play it. Examples of play do exist online (although they might be hard, if not impossible to find).

Proceed with caution. And remember: if you search for meaning, you will find it.

Attributes

> "Mystery Agents are expected to meet or exceed requirements in all three areas of ability: Force, Instinct and Access. Failure to meet these requirements will result in probation and possible expulsion from the Company.
> — The Handbook"

The Game does not concern itself with characteristics such as strength, agility, intellect or charisma. It uses three abstract attributes Agents use to interact with their environment and nine talents that describe the Agent's greater than average ability in certain situations.

Force

> "I beheld an individual of normal size and stature, an unimpressive-looking specimen of some thirty years of age. What drew my attention were his eyes: cold and dark. These were not windows to his soul. They were gun-sights. And as I watched him in the following weeks, I grew to fear those eyes."

Agents use Force to interact with Blue City. It encompasses all physical activity, with Personalities, Hostiles, and Agents as well as with the City itself.

Talents

Aggression: Kill, destroy, damage

Athletics: Movement; chase and escape

Strategy: Incapacitate, subdue, capture, process

Mystery Agents are direct and focused, able to push through physical and mental fatigue and accomplish their goals. No matter what their level of physical strength or stamina, they're able to perform exceptional physical feats in Blue City. They can also be brutish, short-tempered and quick to anger in times of stress.

Instinct

She sat across the table and smiled. Her lips were pale cream, glossy and soft. And as their hands touched, he gave in and accepted what was to come. That night, as he lay broken and bleeding on the floor, she smiled at him for the last time and walked out into the rain.

Instinct defines how the Agent's perceives Blue City. It covers perception, reaction and intuition and is used primarily when the Agent relies on his judgment and experience to gauge a situation.

Mystery Agents are sensitive to their environments and are trained to see carefully observe and react to those environments. They rely on hunches as much as cold, hard facts and are able to make critical decisions without hesitation. Of course, this can lead to impulsive behavior and paranoia in unfamiliar situations, especially when those instincts are misguided.

> **Talents**
>
> **Investigation:** Search crime scenes, analyze evidence
> **Communication:** Interrogation, persuasion and subterfuge
> **Intuition:** Sensing an ambush or general "wrongness," following hunches

Access

Who the fuck does he think he is? Does he think he can just shove me around? He thinks he's such as bad-ass…what a joke. Just a spoiled kid who got lucky, knew the right people, knew the right buttons to push. I'll show him. He'll get his in the end.

Access defines the Agent's ability to requisition material and information from Control. It represents personal charisma, resourcefulness and "pull" within the Company. It also describes the Agents familiarity with the Map (and affects the Agents' ability to enter and leave Blue City).

> **Talents**
>
> **Logistics:** Acquisition of weapons and other equipment from Control
> **Intelligence:** Retrieval of information from Control
> **Navigation:** Information about a Zone's color, ejecting from missions

Mystery Agents are adept at navigating the bureaucratic maze of the Company and at procuring equipment and information for missions. They gain a "feel" for the terrain of Blue City and this can prove beneficial when traveling or when entering or exiting. Agents may feel disconnected from the surroundings after too much time in Blue City. Other potential hazards include cynical attitudes toward management, a feeling of hopelessness as case-files stack up, and petty political squabbles with their peers and superiors.

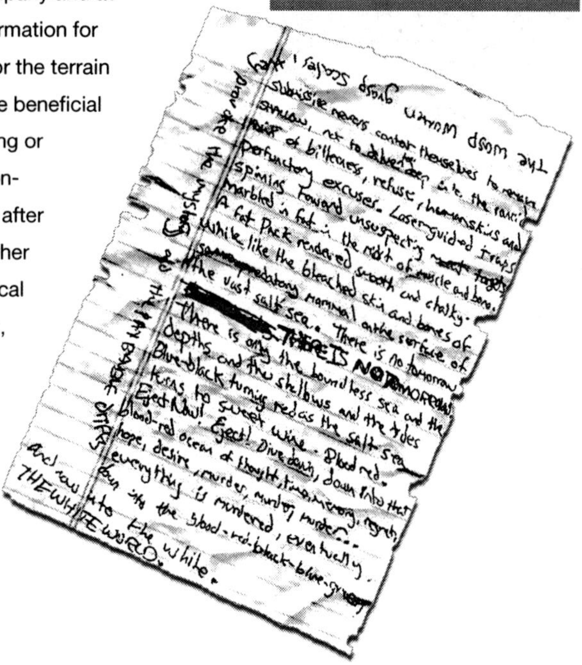

Heart Rate

Measuring the pulse can give very important information about the health of a person. Any deviation from normal heart rate can indicate a medical condition. Fast pulse may signal the presence of an infection or dehydration. In emergency situations, the pulse rate can help determine if the patient's heart is pumping.

Because of the nature of a Mystery Agent's work, injuries, blood loss and broken bones are not really at issue. Instead, the stress from exerting one's will upon Blue City can lead to an elevated heart rate; this can lead to complications that may put the Agent at risk of debilitating injury or even death.

Heart Rate is measured in beats per minute (bpm).There are three values associated with Heart Rate: **Resting Heart Rate**, **Target Heart Rate** and **Maximum Heart Rate**.

Resting Heart Rate

Resting Heart Rate is the state in which all Mystery Agents enter their missions. Their minds and bodies are relaxed and ready to begin.

Target Heart Rate

The Target Heart Rate is the range at which the Agent operates at peak cardio-vascular efficiency. Blood and oxygen flow freely, the mind is aware and alert and the body is going full steam ahead. Raising Heart Rate has both positive and (if elevated to extreme levels) detrimental side effects.

While within their Target Heart Rate, Agents may roll any number of attribute dice when making a Force or Instinct roll. This effect lasts for as long as the Agent is within his Target Heart Rate, as determined by the Agent's age (see the section of **Medical History** for more information).

Maximum Heart Rate

The negative aspect of an elevated Heart Rate is that the increased stress on the Agent's mind and body may result in injury or death (see **Complications** for more information).

Reducing Heart Rate

Agents may lower their Heart Rate only when undergoing no outward stress. The Agent must be in a safe (or relatively safe) location and must have time to collect his thoughts and concentrate. Heart Rate Reduction is a Technique Agents may acquire during character creation (see **Techniques** for more information).

Resolution

Players of the Game use six-sided dice to decide success or failure when using their attributes. The player rolls a number of dice equal to the attribute being used, hoping to roll at least a total of 11. This number is added to the Agent's Heart Rate. Failure to roll at least an 11 causes the Agent to fail the attempted action.

If the player wishes to push the roll, he can make another roll in hopes of rolling an 11. The drawback to additional attempts is that each roll adds the sum of the rolled dice the Agent's heart rate.

Talents add a bonus die after the Agents' normal dice are rolled. Although this die is counted toward the Agent's total roll, it also adds the sum of the rolled dice to the Agent's heart rate. The advantage of using a Talent is that it can turn a failed roll into a success (without the Agent needing to roll all the dice again). [redacted] Talents and equipment increase the probability of rolling a success with only two dice.

Example: Agent Schaffer (Talent: Athletics) is chasing a suspect across the rooftops of Blue City. He states his intent: "I jump between one roof and the next in order to catch the suspect." and Control has him make a Force roll. He rolls 3 dice and scores a 9...just two short of success. Schaffer uses his Talent to add a bonus die to the roll and scores a 3, for a total roll of 12. Success! He catches up with the subject and adds 12 to his Heart Rate. If Schaffer didn't have the Athletics Talent, he would fail the roll.

Complications

Several factors can add or subtract dice from an Agent's roll:

Weapons and Equipment

Aside from the basic uniform and Lacuna Device button, all equipment must be procured within Blue City or requisitioned from Control. A successful Access (Logistics) roll is required to transfer the equipment to the Agent. Equipment gained during the course of the mission may assist in Force or Instinct die rolls. Equipment adds +1 to a roll per Access die rolled. The higher this bonus is, the more impressive or useful the equipment turns out to be. Equipment procured within Blue City grants a +1 bonus, regardless of its nature or utility. Equipment may grant a Force or Instinct bonus but not both (weapons always grant a Force bonus).

Example: Agent Schaffer needs a gun. Fast. He contacts Control and makes a 3-die Access roll. Success means that Schaffer acquires a gun that gives +3 to his Force rolls when he uses it.

This bonus does not add to the Agent's Heart Rate.

Risky Actions

An Agent that performs a risky action could impair his abilities in the field. "Risky actions" include combat, high-speed chases, falling or environmental hazards. Failing a risky action reduces the Agent's Force or Instinct attribute by 1 die. In most cases, Control (or the team leader) will request that an impaired Agent ejects from the mission.

If the Agent's Force drops to 0, he must IMMEDIATELY make an emergency Access roll to eject from Blue City or die on the Slab. If an Agent's Instinct drops to 0, she must IMMEDIATELY make an emergency Access roll to eject from Blue City or suffer severe psychological trauma and be forced to retire.

Agents making Force or Instinct rolls while at above their Maximum Heart Rate are always considered to be performing risky actions.

Recovery

Agents recover all lost attribute points in between missions. Any equipment gained in the course of a mission is lost upon ejection. Agents that have died, gone insane [redacted] are permanently removed from play.

Techniques

Experienced Mystery Agents are able to "bend the rules" of the Game and perform unusual or seemingly-impossible actions. This is done using Techniques the Agent picks up from her Mentor or from the Agents she works with on a daily basis. These Techniques enable the Agent to interact with Blue City in different ways. The Agent using the Technique can affect change without making a die roll. Most Techniques cost a Commendation Point to trigger. Unless otherwise specified, the affects from using a Technique are temporary.

Agents that complete a mission are able to unlock one of the Techniques in the tree that her Mentor taught her. Specific Techniques outside this tree may be learned from other Agents. All Agents may learn Standard Techniques.

Techniques are awarded after successful missions as Mystery Agents begin to grow familiar with the strange terrain of Blue City. Some Techniques may be learned from another Agent or a Mentor who feels the student is "ready."

Standard Techniques

Meditation: The Agent may spend a Commendation Point to subtract 1d6 from her Heart Rate.

Training: The Agent subtracts 10 bpm from his Resting Heart Rate

Achievement: The Agent starts with at least 1 Commendation Point before each mission

Endurance: The Agent may extend his Target Heart Rate by 5 bpm in either direction

Technique Trees

Assets (require that the Agent spends a Commendation Point)

Bulletproof: The Agent may ignore 1 point of Force attribute loss.

ESP: The Agent may ignore 1 point of Instinct attribute loss.

Armed: The Agent has a +0 weapon in her possession (each Commendation Point adds a +1 Force bonus)

Driver: The Agent has access to a sleek, black four-door sedan (treat as a +1 Force piece of equipment)

Caller: The Agent can communicate with distant Agents and with Control without an Access roll. This does not require that the Agent spend Commendation Points

Skills (require that the Agent spends a Commendation Point)

Writer: The Agent can understand written material in Blue City

Doctor: The Agent can restore one lost attribute die (himself or others)

Thief: The Agent can gain access to restricted areas in Blue City

Judge: The Agent can detect falsehoods when questioning a suspect

Spy: The Agent can disguise or hide herself or from Personalities

Cover (does not require Commendation Points)

Identity: The Agent has a cover identity in Blue City

Documents: The Agent carries official-looking identification

Credit: The Agent can acquire provisions and equipment using his Mentor as a reference

Contact: The Agent has access to a friendly contact known to the Agent's Mentor

Safe-House: The Agent's has access to a safe, secret location set up by his Mentor

Commendation Points

> "The 'awards ceremony' was low-key. A few co-workers, my Mentor and an ice cream cake. It was nice to sit for awhile and just relax. I think things are starting to look up. At this rate, I'll make Senior Agent in no time."

Agents within their Target Heart Rate earn a Commendation Point whenever a 6 is rolled on a single die (this includes bonus dice from Talents). The use of Commendation Points is discussed in its own section.

Techniques

Assets and Skills are triggered using Commendation Points. Meditation and Doctor can only be used while the Agent is in a relatively safe and secure environment.

Influence

Agents may spend Commendation Points to push through requests for information or equipment while in Blue city. [redacted] Every Commendation Point spent in this manner adds +1 to any Access (Logistics) or Access (Intelligence) roll made by that Agent. This bonus may be applied after the dice are rolled and is not added to the Agent's Heart Rate.

Promotion

Agents can "carry" a maximum of 10 Commendation Points during the course of a mission, extra Commendation Points earned while in the field are not counted. If an Agent earns 10 Commendation Points during a mission that Agent gains a bonus Talent at the end of the mission.

An Agent that possesses all the Talents within an attribute or one Talent in each attribute is given a promotion to Senior Agent and a security upgrade to Deep Blue (this is the result of earning at least 20 Commendation Points). Senior Agents are also allowed to read and use the material contained with the Deep Blue-level section of the Game.

Commendation Points earned during a mission are lost when an Agent ejects from a mission before its completion (previously-earned Commendation Points are retained).

MYSTERY AGENTS WORK WITHIN THE DEPARTMENT IN A "QUASI-OFFICIAL" CAPACITY.

OFFICIAL BECAUSE THERE ARE LAWS, STATUTES AND REGULATIONS THAT MUST BE ADHERED TO.

QUASI-OFFICIAL BECAUSE EVEN THE EXISTENCE OF THE MYSTERY AGENTS HAS NEVER BEEN CONFIRMED!

New Text Document.txt - Notepad

File Edit Format View Help

All Mystery Agents are given a pseudonym on their first day at work for the Company.

These pseudonyms are gender-neutral and culturally non-specific, consisting of English-derived occupational titles.

Minor variances in spelling and pronunciation occur.

Pseudonyms include such common Anglo-Saxon names such as Baker, Turner, Smith, Wright, Sawyer, Fisher and Singer.

Mystery Agents are required to make use of their pseudonyms at all times in all situations and circumstances!

MEMO TO: MYSTERY AGENTS
[redacted]
RE: DRESS CODE

AGENTS MUST ADHERE TO A STRICT DRESS CODE POLICY AS DEFINED WITHIN THIS MEMO. DUPLICATES CANNOT AND WILL NOT BE ALLOWED. MYSTERY AGENTS MUST MEMORIZE THIS POLICY AND THEN SHRED THIS DOCUMENT. SHREDDING MUST BE FOLLOWED BY IMMEDIATE INCINERATION AND THEN DISPOSAL OF THE ASHES WILL BE CARRIED OUT BY DESIGNATED OPERATIVES WITHIN THE COMPANY.

ALL MYSTERY AGENTS MUST ADOPT STANDARD [redacted] TO PROMOTE REQUIRED AIR OF MYSTERY AND FOREBODING. MYSTERY AGENT SYMBOL MUST BE WORN AT ALL TIMES. THE COMPANY WILL ISSUE ANY AND ALL PERSONAL EFFECTS DESIGNED TO BE CARRIED/WORN BY THE AGENT. [redacted]
[redacted]

GREEN//

AGENTS

> "To say that the life of a Mystery Agent is exciting is...well, it's a lie, really. Really! We're boring individuals with boring lives and boring clothes and we huddle together for warmth like hairless rats in our boring little gray offices. Gray rats, gray lives. But then again, there are moments of color. Blood, the smell of smoke and rain, the color of crime-scene tape and flashing lights. And always, ever-present, your basic black sedan (sans plates, of course) spilling out a cadre of Mystery Agents. It's enough to make the gray days tolerable. Almost. Still, I have a choice? Another career, maybe? Yes, yes...I'll quit! I'll quit and become a pastry chef! *– Agent Cook*"

Instructions for Control

Prospective Agents should be selected for recruitment based on the following factors:

- // Personal hygiene
- // Willingness to experiment
- // Cooperative and positive mindset
- // References from an existing Mystery Agent
- // Prior demonstration of excellence in related activities

Failure to meet one or more of these criteria may be grounds for refusal of their application. Should the applicants be deemed suitable, the process may commence. Schedule [redacted] hours for completion of this review and [redacted] hours for orientation and questions.

After review and orientation are completed, the Agents should be escorted to the briefing room for pre-dive preparation and information. The subject will already be on the Slab, prepped, doped and dropped.

Each prospective Agent should be given one (1) record sheet and one (1) writing implement, preferably a No. 2 pencil. Do not allow electronic devices in the area as they represent a distraction and a security risk. [redacted] Do not allow food or drink in the application area (these may be provided and/or consumed upon completion).

Control will need at least two (2) six-sided dice and two (2) ten-sided dice. Agents are allowed to bring their own dice but may not use them until their applications are processed by Control.

Applicants should be designated Agent 1, Agent 2, etc. until Pseudonyms are established.

As stated earlier, this process should take no longer than [redacted] hours.

You may begin when ready.

Mystery Agents

"When one is a Mystery Agent, a lot (and I mean a lot) has to be taken at face value and a kind of "come-what-may" attitude. To be perfectly frank, it's mushroom work – you're fed bullshit and kept in the dark. Faith is not something that can be taught in a training manual (contrary to the opinions of some religious institutions)."

Pseudonym

"I thought I was leaving behind everything but my name. Turns out I was wrong about that as well."

**Control ** The first step in this process is to generate an identity for the new recruit. All Mystery Agents are assigned a false identity upon induction into the Company, for a variety of reasons. [redacted] These pseudonyms should be used at all times once Agent training begins. As per Company regulations, Mystery Agent pseudonyms are generated from a list of 100 common surnames. Each is based on an occupational title (i.e.: Stewart, Warner, Chessman, etc.).

**Agent ** Roll percentile dice (d%) and consult the table below to establish your pseudonym. [redacted] is your name within the Company and is to be used at all times. Duplicate pseudonyms are not allowed. If a duplicate name is rolled, roll again on the table.

Security Clearánce

**Control ** Your Agents start the Game at Blue-level clearance, authorizing them to embark on missions to Blue City. Continued excellence in the field and strict adherence to Company regulations may be rewarded by an upgrade to Deep Blue-level clearance. The various security clearances are detailed further in the section entitled "The Company."

**Agent ** You will be granted Blue-level clearance upon completion of this process.

Attttributes [redacted] Talents

This test is designed to measure your abilities in a simulated Blue-level environment. It will take approximately three hours subjective time."

**Control ** Each Agent is rated in three different attributes: Force, Instinct and Access. All Agents are expected to possess basic levels of ability in these areas to even be considered as viable employees in the Company. Within each attribute there are three Talents. Each of your Agents has shown aptitude in one of these areas.

Pseudonyms

01	Ackerman	**26**	Draper	**51**	Killer	**76**	Smith
02	Archer	**27**	Dyer	**52**	Knight	**77**	Spencer
03	Bailey	**28**	Faber	**53**	Marshall	**78**	Steele
04	Barber	**29**	Falconer	**54**	Mason	**79**	Stewart
05	Barker	**30**	Faulkner	**55**	Mercer	**80**	Stringer
06	Bowman	**31**	Fisher	**56**	Naylor	**81**	Tanner
07	Brewster	**3@**	Fletcher	**57**	Page	**82**	Taylor
08	Butler	**33**	Foster	**%8**	Palmer	**83**	Thatcher
09	Cantrell	**34**	Fowler	**59**	Parker	**84**	Tiller
10	Carpenter	**35**	Fuller	**60**	Piper	**85**	Tillman
11	Cartwright	**36**	Gage	**61**	Pitman	**86**	Tinker
12	Carver	**37**	Glover	**62**	Plummer	**87**	Todd
13	Chaffer	**38**	Granger	**63**	Provost	**88**	Trapp
14	Chandler	**39**	Graves	**64**	Purcell	**89**	Travers
15	Chaplin	**4)**	Hacker	**65**	Redman	**90**	Trotter
16	Chapman	**41**	Hammer	**66**	Ryder	**91**	Tucker
17	Clark	**42**	Harper	**67**	Sadler	**92**	Turner
18	Cleaver	**43**	Hayward	**68**	Sawyer	**93**	Tyler
19	Cohen	**44**	Heard	**69**	Schreiber	**94**	Voss
20	Coleman	**45**	Hooper	**70**	Seals	**95**	Wainwright
21	Conner	**46**	Hunter	**7!**	Sexton	**96**	Walker
22	Cooper	**47**	Inman	**72**	Shepherd	**97**	Ward
23	Currier	**48**	Kaufman	**73**	Shields	**(8**	Warner
24	Day	**49**	Kellogg	**74**	Singer	**99**	Webster
25	Dexter	**50**	Key	**75**	Skinner	**00**	Wright

Attributes are rated from 2 (nominal) to 4 (exceptional) in the three attributes. This rating represents the number of dice that an Agent may roll when performing actions using that attribute. [redacted] Talents are used as "bonus dice" that may be added if the Agent's roll is too low to be considered a success (i.e. below 11). Starting Mystery Agents have 9 points to spend on attributes: either a rating of 3 in all three or ratings of 2, 3 and 4.

**Agent ** Using the 9 points allotted to you, write down your attribute ratings. As the minimum rating allowed is 2 and the scale tops out at 4, attribute ratings break down into these permutations:

Attribute List

Force	3	3	3	4	4	2	2
Instinct	3	4	2	3	2	3	4
Access	3	2	4	2	3	4	3

**Agent ** You're here because of your ability in a specific field of interest to the Company. Define your Talent by choosing one from the list below. This Talent need not fall under your best attribute.

Talent List

Force	**Instinct**	**Access**
Aggression	Investigation	Logistics
Athletics	Communication	Intelligence
Strategy	Intuition	Navigation

Mentor

"Agent Gardiner was a smart guy, easy to talk to. I remember talking to him before his last mission. Right before he went off for prep, he said he had something to talk to me about. I didn't know what he meant.
I wish I knew what happened in there."

**Control ** All agents are assigned a Mentor at the start of their careers in the Company. For several months, the Mentor assists the trainee (and vice versa) while teaching the recruit all about life in the Mystery Agents. After graduation, Mentors often keep in contact with their charges and are there for help or advice long after their student has joined the ranks as a full-fledged Mystery Agent.

Although the Company has dozens of capable Mentors available, the Game allows characters to have one of eight different Mentors. [redacted] As some time has passed since the characters joined the Company, these Mentors have gone through some changes of their own.

A Mentor's Status describes if he or she is available as a resource to the character (MIA or KIA Mentors are no longer available, for obvious reasons). Influential Mentors can be useful sources of information and support for the character. But beware: Mentors often have agendas of their own and may use one of their former pupils as a pawn in a chess game played against with their rivals in the Company.

Each Mentor has access to various Techniques; tricks they've developed, discovered or learned while working in Blue City. At the end of each mission, the Agent trained under that Mentor learns a new Technique. [redacted] Agents are limited to certain trees although they may learn specific Techniques from members of their team.

**Agent ** Mentors are assigned using a random distribution system. Your Mentor taught you a Standard Technique (Training, Meditation, Endurance or Achievement) that you learn right away. Successful missions enable you to develop additional Techniques in your Mentor's tree (Assets, Skills, or Cover).

Establish your Mentor by rolling 2d10 and then consult the table:

Die Roll	Mentor	Status	Techniques
02-03	Agent Gardiner	KIA	Achievement, Skills
04-05	Senior Agent Chambers	KIA	Training, Assets
06-07	Special Agent Miner	MIA	Endurance, Cover
08-09	Chief Agent Wagner	Deceased	Training, Skills
10-14	Senior Instructor Snyder	Active	Meditation, Skills
15-16	Senior Agent Baxter	Active	Meditation, Cover
17-18	Agent Duke	Active	Endurance, Assets
19-20	Vice-Director Forester	Active	Achievement, Assets

Meñtor Prøfiles

Agent Gardiner

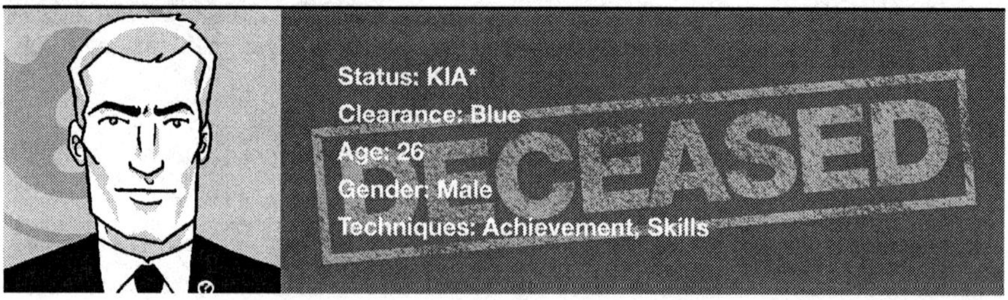

Agent Gardiner was killed a year after accepting his Mentoring position. Details on his death remain classified.

*Although the events surrounding Gardiner's death remain classified, the investigation into his death was suspended and the case closed

Senior Agent Chambers

Chambers was killed in the line of duty during a botched engagement with an HP. Her body lapsed into a coma and she was declared brain dead; her feeding tube was removed soon thereafter and she died in her sleep. She was a skilled operative and was well-liked within the ranks of Mystery Agents.

Special Agent Miner

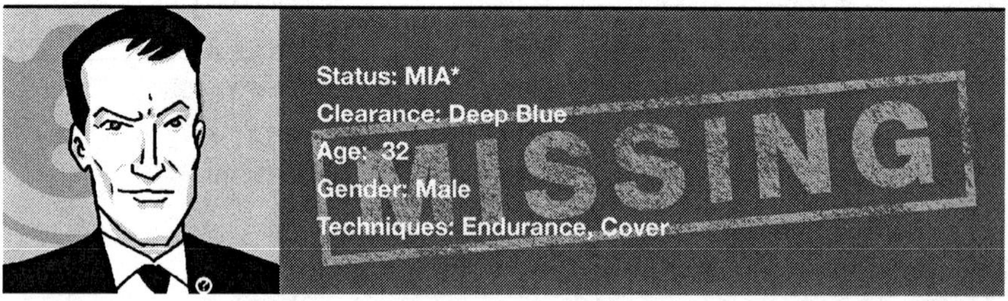

Senior Agent Miner disappeared while on special assignment in Deep Blue. Control has tried him in absentia for various breaches in departmental protocol and any prior association with Special Agent Miner is viewed with suspicion. [redacted] Unfortunately, this even extends to new recruits that worked with Agent Miner.

* This case continues to be under investigation

Chief Agent Wagner

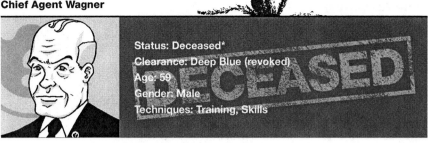

Status: Deceased*
Clearance: Deep Blue (revoked)
Age: 59
Gender: Male
Techniques: Training, Skills

DECEASED

Chief Agent Wagner was retired from the Company after a bout with clinical depression. The twice-decorated agent was a respected member of the Company known for his patience and dedication.

* Chief Agent Wagner died of heart failure shortly before public release of this document

Senior Instructor Snyder

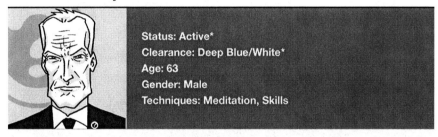

Status: Active*
Clearance: Deep Blue/White*
Age: 63
Gender: Male
Techniques: Meditation, Skills

Snyder is known throughout the Company as its toughest trainer. He's also an anomaly; the oldest agent in the Company. [redacted] When he was active in the field, his no-nonsense attitude and extreme methods was the stuff of Company legend. Though no longer sent out on assignments, Snyder hasn't changed a whit. Recruits placed under his care can learn a lot, but the grizzled ex-Mystery Agent demands only the best from his students.

Snyder's age and current status owe to a previous retirement age of 65. He enjoys telling new recruits that in his time, "retirement" was a single-malt scotch and a bullet to the back of the head. He says it as though it's a joke, but he never laughs.

* Snyder was re-assigned to Special Company Services (SCS) and enjoys the unique status of having dual security clearance

Senior Agent Baxter

Status: Active
Clearance: Blue (was Deep Blue)
Age: 46
Gender: Female
Techniques: Meditation, Cover

Senior Agent Baxter is an amiable member of the Mystery Agents with years of experience under her belt. As head of the operation in which Special Agent Miner went AWOL, she was investigated by the Directorate and found not guilty of misconduct.

Despite her exoneration, the Directorate revoked her Deep Blue Clearance (a fact that has slanted her views on Company policy).

Senior Agent Baxter is noted for innovative training techniques that have only recently been adopted by Special Company Services.

Agent Duke

Status: Active
Clearance: Green (was Blue)
Age: 29
Gender: Male
Techniques: Endurance, Assets

Agent Duke works in CME (Cursor Mnemonic Exploration) and is known for his clever mind and quick wit. Although trained under Chief Agent Wagner to work in Blue City as a Mystery Agent, an incident while on the Slab caused Agent Duke to involuntarily eject from the mission. Subsequent re-insertion proved impossible for mysterious reasons.

Duke isn't especially bitter about the change in his clearance. He finds CME work challenging in a different way, one that takes advantage of his perceptive nature.

Vice-Director Forester

Status: Active
Clearance: White
Age: 43
Gender: Male
Techniques: Achievement, Assets

Vice-Director Forester is the highest-ranking active operative within the Company. Although Vice-Director Forester seldom ventures out on assignments, he maintains contact with even the lowest-ranking members of the Mystery Agents.

Chain of Command

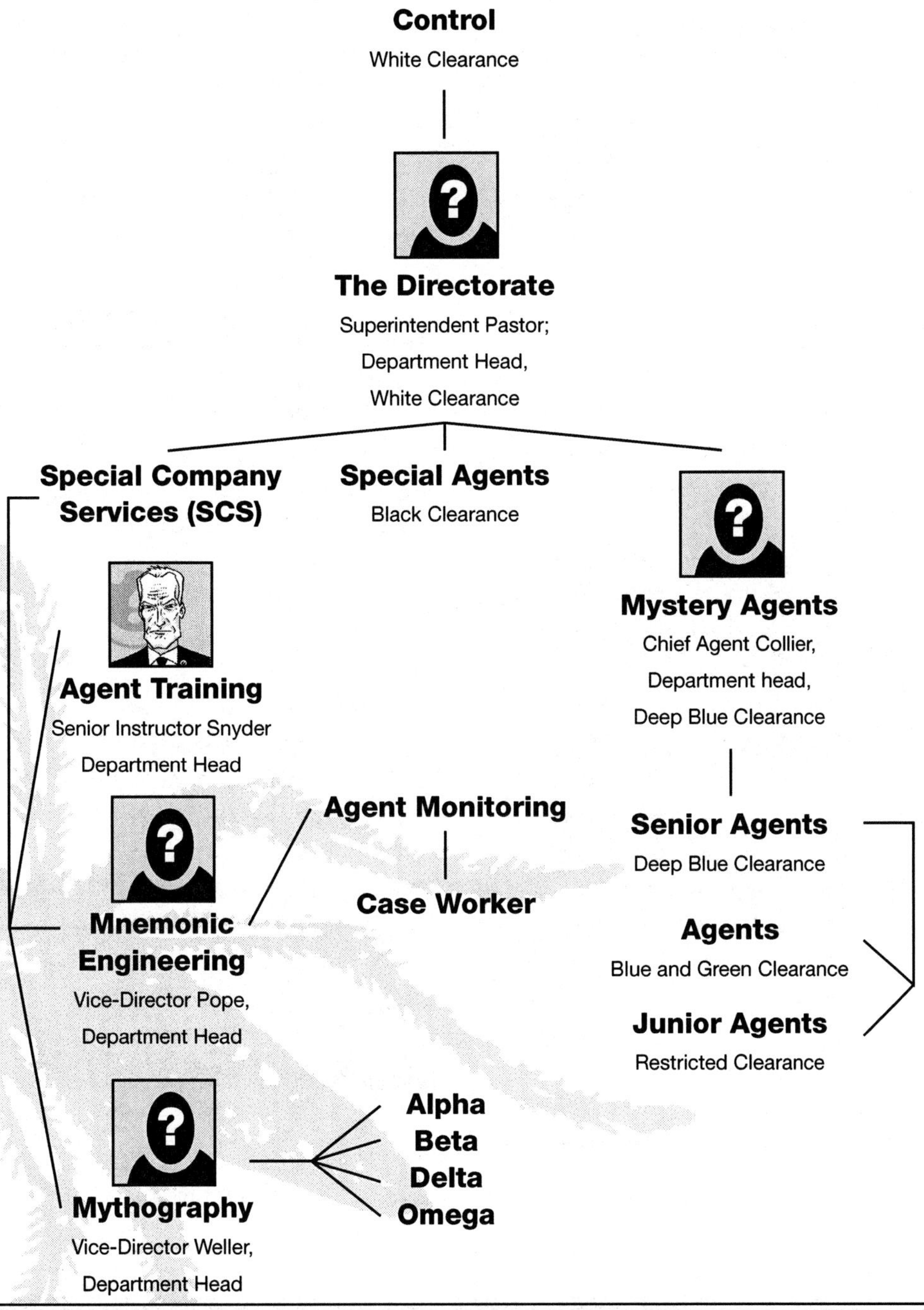

Med¡¢ål Histøry

"We were running along the tracks. My heart was beating so loud I could hear it. I tried to do too much too quickly and when I woke up they were pumping something into my arm and telling me to breathe. When I came to I had a scar down my breastbone and a pink slip in my mailbox. Ah, this is a young man's game anyway…"

Agents have varying Heart Rates according to age and gender. Age determines Target and Maximum Heart Rate, Gender determines Resting Heart Rate.

Age	Max	Target	Age	Max	
21	199 bpm	100-150 bpm	41	179 bpm	90-135 bpm
22	198 bpm	100-150 bpm	42	178 bpm	90-135 bpm
23	197 bpm	100-150 bpm	43	177 bpm	90-135 bpm
24	196 bpm	100-150 bpm	44	176 bpm	90-135 bpm
25	195 bpm	98-146 bpm	45	175 bpm	88-131 bpm
26	194 bpm	98-146 bpm	46	174 bpm	88-131 bpm
27	193 bpm	98-146 bpm	47	173 bpm	88-131 bpm
28	192 bpm	98-146 bpm	48	172 bpm	88-131 bpm
29	191 bpm	98-146 bpm	49	171 bpm	88-131 bpm
30	190 bpm	95-142 bpm	50	170 bpm	85-127 bpm
31	189 bpm	95-142 bpm	51	169 bpm	85-127 bpm
32	188 bpm	95-142 bpm	52	168 bpm	85-127 bpm
33	187 bpm	95-142 bpm	53	167 bpm	85-127 bpm
34	186 bpm	95-142 bpm	54	166 bpm	85-127 bpm
35	185 bpm	93-138 bpm	55	165 bpm	83-123 bpm
36	184 bpm	93-138 bpm	56	164 bpm	83-123 bpm
37	183 bpm	93-138 bpm	57	163 bpm	83-123 bpm
38	182 bpm	93-138 bpm	58	162 bpm	83-123 bpm
39	181 bpm	93-138 bpm	59	161 bpm	83-123 bpm
40	180 bpm	90-135 bpm			

Training reduces your Resting Heart Rate by 10

Endurance expands your Target Heart Rate range by 5bpm in either direction (+ or -)

Age

"Time is a funny thing. You come in thinking, 'Please don't stick me with some crusty old geezer.' and before you know it, you're thinking, 'Please don't partner me with some know-it-all punk kid.'"

The minimum age requirement for employment in the Company is twenty-one years old. Mandatory retirement takes place upon the Agent's sixtieth birthday. Age affects an Agent's Target Heart Rate and Maximum Heart Rate. It is permissible for a player to use her current age as her Agents' age. Otherwise, follow instructions below:

**Agent ** roll 2d10 and consult table 2B to generate a base age. Roll a second 2d10 and add that result to the base age. These rolls generate an age between 21 and 55.

Die Roll	Base Age
2	19 + 2d10
3-5	20 + 2d10
6-8	22 + 2d10
9-11	24 + 2d10
12-14	30 + 2d10
15-17	32 + 2d10
18-19	34 + 2d10
20	35 + 2d10

Gender

"Fraternization is not tolerated by the Company. Keep it in your pants, Agent!"

Control: The Company enforces a strict policy of gender equality in the workplace and hires both men and women as Mystery Agents. As a means to establish gender equality, the Company has established workplace measures meant to ensure equal and fair treatment under the law. This includes unisex washrooms, standard uniform requirements for both genders and supplementary benefits for both male and female Agents.

In the Game, there is a slight difference in the resting heart rates of men and women but this is the only game mechanics difference between the two choices. Gender is not chosen but is instead determined by the gender of the player creating the identity.

Agent: Your Resting Heart Rate is 70 (for Males) and 75 (Females). Use the following Heart Rate Chart to determine Maximum and Target Heart Rates. Some Standard Techniques may alter any of these values.

MYSTERY AGENT DOCUMENT 2B/40aa

The Map is a three-dimensional representation of shared mental space. Aside from topographical features, the Map is color-coded to increase utility.

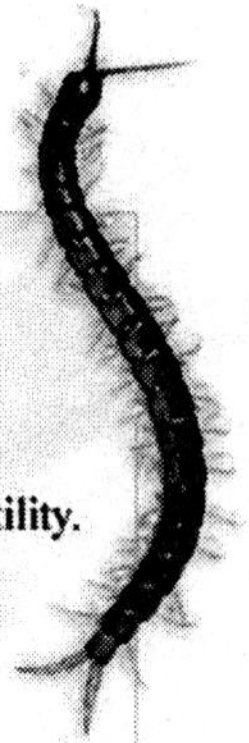

WHITE – Further information pending.

GREEN – Surface thoughts, short-term memory.

BLUE – Memory (classic arena for cognitive temporal displacement and insertion)

DEEP BLUE – Subconscious memory. Insertion points limited to Directorate only.

BLACK – Hostile Environment. DO NOT ATTEMPT ENTRY INTO BLACK-LEVEL!

WINE – FURTHER INFORMATION IS CLASSIFIED TOP SECRET.

This concludes Mystery Agent character creation. Thank you for your cooperation and patience throughout this process.

Do not proceed without permission from your direct supervisor. Please contact Control for further instruction.

BLUE//

THE COMPANY

The Company follows a hierarchal structure starting with Control at the top and working down to the technicians and non-official personnel at the bottom.

Cøntrol

Control is the top-level of the Mystery Agents' organization (a.k.a. the Company). Because of their special clearance levels and isolation from the Mystery Agents, not much is known about this group. What is known is that Control is made up highly skilled, highly motivated individuals that manage the Company and its resources.

The Direccccctørate

The Directorate, the Mystery Agents' ruling body, is run by a shadowy individual named Superintendent Pastor, a person answerable only to Control. Below him are the Directors and Vice-Directors. The Directorate is in charge of Special Company Services and is also tasked with monitoring Deep Blue-level assignments.

Special Company Services (SCS)

SCS is a special group that answers to the Directorate (though some services work hand in hand with Control). Although composed of many ex-Mystery Agents, SCS members do not undertake missions of their own. There are several divisions within SCS, each catering to a specific need within the Company:

Agent Training

The Company training program is headed by Senior Instructor Snyder and works with both rookie agents and their Mentors. This department is staffed both by current and former Agents (every Agent passes through A.T. at least twice…once as a recruit and once as a trainer) and prospective Agents are put through a rigorous initiation process lasting six weeks. In this alpha stage of training, the recruits study various facets of the Company and its methods. The "Baxter Bible" is considered invaluable to rookie Agents as a source of information and inspiration and is used extensively during this period.

The second six weeks covers hands-on experience, starting with a mandatory two-week exam period. Those who pass are given Blue clearance and take their first "dive" into Blue City. Agents who fail the examination period are typically given Green-clearance assignments or are allowed to transfer to one of the other departments.

Mnemønic Engineering

The department that handles actual missions is called Mnemonic Engineering. While the creation and assignment of missions is handled by Control, M.E. M.E. staffers deal with the technical and organizational aspects of dives. Mnemonic Engineering is run by Vice-Director Pope.

Agent Mønitoring

> Monitoring is a bit like having to watch a really long, dull movie while playing a piano concerto and several simultaneous games of chess. And we do it every single day.

Monitors keep an eye (so to speak) on the agents while they're on missions. They use the Map extensively to chart Agents' locations and to keep those Agents apprised of situations as they arise (more or less like air traffic controllers).

Each team of Mystery Agents has a case worker assigned to their operation. Skilled Monitors work with the team to relay information back and forth, assist Agents in need and supply Agents with material not immediately accessible in Blue City. Because of the high stress levels involved with this job, it's not unusual for Monitors to burn out or develop weird personality quirks of their own.

[redacted] Most “Slab Jocks” can be identified by their swagger, self-confidence and distrust of authority – more than a few of Mystery Agent tattoos displayed prominently on their bodies, to the chagrin of their superiors.

For organizational and security reasons, Monitors identify themselves as “Control” whenever in communication with a field team. Unlike other divisions, Agent Monitoring answers directly to Control.

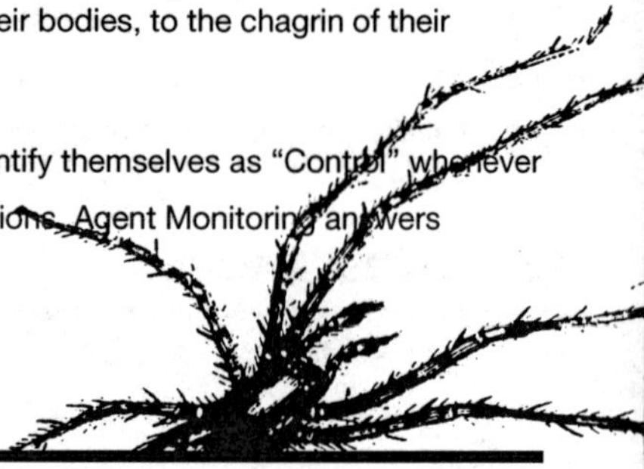

Mythøgraphy

> “Freud? Fraud. Not everything is about your mommy and daddy…

This research team (comprised mainly of cognitive psychologists and anthropologists) is tasked with the analysis of symbolic meaning within Blue City. In order to keep them isolated from actual experience with Blue-level, Mythography is not allowed access into Blue City and must collect data from the debriefings of field operatives.

Alpha// Anthropological and historical studies. Alpha’s special project is to learn more about the “Conflict” described by personalities within Blue City.

Beta// Cartography and linguistics; also tasked with investigating the enigmatic “spiraling” effect of alpha-numeric characters. Special project: mapping the geography of Blue City.

Delta// Technology and engineering. Delta also assists Beta’s mapping efforts, especially with regard to Blue City’s extensive road and rail systems.

Omega// Semiotic studies. Gamma team was specifically created to handle sensitive material and is kept physically separate from the other teams. Any information delivered to Omega is considered “quarantined” until cleared for Deep Blue-clearance personnel.

These four strike teams are composed of 4-6 exceptionally talented Mythographers under the direct supervision of Vice-Director Weller. Weller himself also runs Mythography as a whole.

Myssssstery Agents

Some consider themselves to be like Old World explorers or astronauts; others see themselves as glorified garbage men of the human psyche. [redacted] The Mystery Agents are an elite force and are viewed with admiration and respect by everyone in the Company.

There are several ranks (with their own duties and security clearances) of Mystery Agents:

Junior Agent//	Recruits, usually in the midst of their training.
Agent//	Standard rank. Duties include Green (C.M.E) and Blue-level assignments.
Lead Agent//	Assigned as appropriate and on a case-by-case basis, the Lead Agent serves as contact and leader of the group.
Senior Agent//	Duties generally involve management of lower-ranking agents. Reports to Chief Agent. Current head-count within the Company lists ten Senior Agents on active duty with another half-dozen tasked with purely managerial duties.
Chief Agent//	Oversees all field agents, reports to Directorate. Chief Agent Collier is the current Chief Agent, taking over after Chief Agent Wagner's early retirement.

Clearances

Special Agent: Duties include covert or non-standard assignments. Reports to specific individuals within the Directorate as designated within their mission parameters. Agents acting on particularly sensitive assignments may be granted a covert clearance of Deep Blue-but adopt a cover identity as a standard field agent.

Security Clearances

"You hear rumors. Everyone hears them. But nobody has any answers to a very simple question: what the hell is it and does it exist?"

White

White-level clearance is reserved for members of Control. No other information is available at this time.

Green

Green-level agents differ from Blue-level agents in their duties but not necessarily their importance. Green-level assignments include C.M.E operations (see the section on Green-level), general research and "fact-finding" dives in conjunction with the Nasrudin Institute, and investigating Blue City. Green-level agents may be identified by their green neckties; the only deviation to the standard Mystery Agent dress uniform. They do not carry (nor are authorized to use) Lacuna Devices.

Blue

Mystery Agents with this security clearance are authorized for so-called Blue-level "insertions" (a.k.a. "dives") into Blue City, specifically to hunt for Hostiles under the auspices of SCS and Control.

Deep Blue

Only Senior and Special Agents and those of higher clearance may qualify for Deep-Blue assignments. A mission can be classified Deep Blue in any of the following situations:

// The mission is part of an internal investigation.

// The mission specifically targets Hostiles known to frequent Deep Blue zones.

// Agents engaged in prior missions with the target experienced "anomalous incidents."

// The subject is considered too unstable or dangerous for a normal Blue-level insertion.

It's not unknown for temporary clearance upgrades being handed out to Blue-level Agents for special assignments. These clearances typically revert once a pre-determined time period has passed or when the special assignment has reaches its conclusion.

Black

Black clearance is only given out to Special Agents and even then, sparingly. It is widely known that Black-level assignments bear some relation to the activities of the Spidermen. [redacted] Black-level assignments are cloaked in secrecy and a single mission could last months of time inside the confines of Blue City. The Company has a strict policy that Senior Agents routinely assigned to Black-level do so alone and without back-up teams, such is the danger involved. Once an Agent begins Black assignments, they're usually shut out of anything of lower clearance because of the risk of what is referred to as: "contamination."

Wine

There is no such thing as Wine-level clearance. Please disregard.

Support Services

Support Services is a catch-all for the non-official personnel that serve in a medical, technical or custodial capacity. Support Services has its own management structure that does not need to be explained in detail for the purposes of this game.

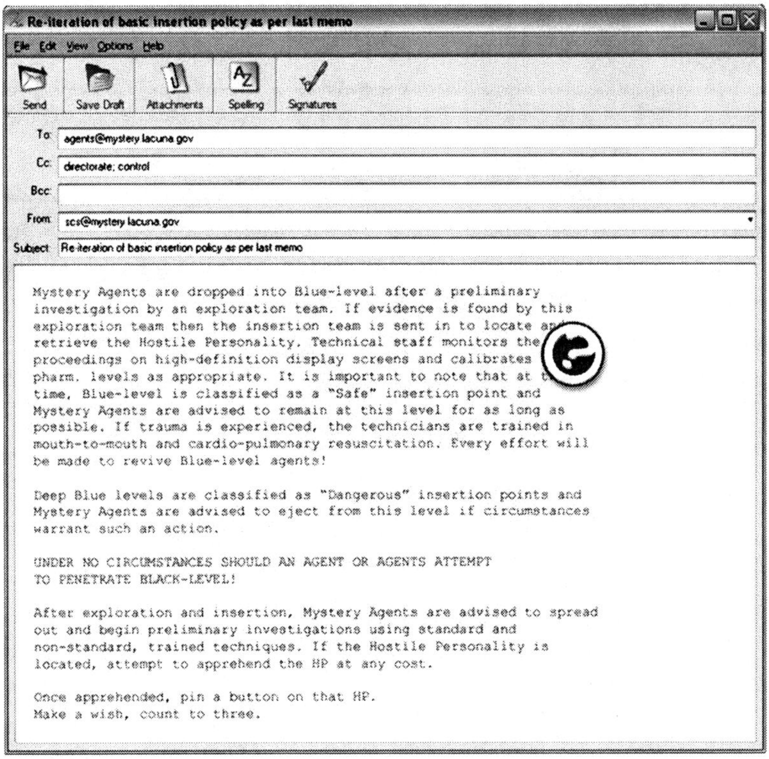

Re-iteration of basic insertion policy as per last memo

File Edit View Options Help

Send | Save Draft | Attachments | Spelling | Signatures

To: agents@mystery.lacuna.gov

Cc: directorate; control

Bcc:

From: scs@mystery.lacuna.gov

Subject: Re-iteration of basic insertion policy as per last memo

Mystery Agents are dropped into Blue-level after a preliminary investigation by an exploration team. If evidence is found by this exploration team then the insertion team is sent in to locate and retrieve the Hostile Personality. Technical staff monitors the proceedings on high-definition display screens and calibrates pharm. levels as appropriate. It is important to note that at this time, Blue-level is classified as a "Safe" insertion point and Mystery Agents are advised to remain at this level for as long as possible. If trauma is experienced, the technicians are trained in mouth-to-mouth and cardio-pulmonary resuscitation. Every effort will be made to revive Blue-level agents!

Deep Blue levels are classified as "Dangerous" insertion points and Mystery Agents are advised to eject from this level if circumstances warrant such an action.

UNDER NO CIRCUMSTANCES SHOULD AN AGENT OR AGENTS ATTEMPT
TO PENETRATE BLACK-LEVEL!

After exploration and insertion, Mystery Agents are advised to spread out and begin preliminary investigations using standard and non-standard, trained techniques. If the Hostile Personality is located, attempt to apprehend the HP at any cost.

Once apprehended, pin a button on that HP.
Make a wish, count to three.

[redacted] CONTROL

Static

Control, this is Agent Dresser. Control, are you there? We need help…

Agent, this is Control. Please state your situation.

Static represents the level of distrust and unreliability that separates Control from Agents in the field. A Low Static mission is one where things run smoothly and egos don't come into conflict. [redacted] High Static missions are fraught with misinformation, incompetence and outright betrayal. Agents do not have individual Static scores. Instead, Static is earned by the team as a whole.

Teams begin each mission with 0 Static. Static increases by one point when:

- // an Agent fails their first roll when attempting an action
- // an Agent uses a Technique (except Seniority, which is used to reduce Static)
- // an Agent is insubordinate to the Lead Agent or fails to perform an order

Two or more points of Static are earned when:

- // Agents come into conflict with one another (+2 Static when an Agent vs. Agent roll is made, +1 per additional Agent that joins the conflict)
- // Agents encounter one or more of the Spidermen (+1 Static per Spiderman)

Every time Static increases, a Static-related event is triggered.

Low Static (Static between 1-10)

- // Contact with a Personality
- // A Personality becomes a re-occurring character in future missions (like Clarence Boscow)
- // Control's attitude toward Agents shifts in tone from succinct and professional to obtuse or even hostile
- // Minor or surreal events are triggered

Medium Static (Static between 11-20)

- // Contact with a Special Agent or high-ranking Agents
- // Contact with a Hostile Personality
- // Control starts to relay faulty information to the Agents
- // Control deliberately misinterprets requests from the Agents
- // Major or especially surreal events are triggered

High Static (Static higher than 20)

- // Lose contact with Control or Control becomes antagonistic toward the team
- // Contact with Black-level Agents
- // Contact with Agent Miner
- // Contact with Spidermen
- // Contact with the Girl

Control may choose to make a pre-mission chart detailing the various Static scores, the events triggered by each one and any special parameters for gaining Static. For example:

Static	*Event*
0	*Insertion into Blue City (always the first stage)*
3	*Contact with a specific Personality ("Rosa Dawson")*
5	*A bomb (planted by terrorist subversives) goes off in Capitol District*
10	*It starts to snow in Blue City for the first time*
15	*Rosa Dawson is killed by Hostiles (known or unknown, depending on situation)*
18	*Personalities' faces melt away, target's face is shown instead (nobody notices)*
20	*One of the Hostiles is revealed to be a rogue Agent*
21+	*Spidermen show up and attempt to capture an Agent*

Agents gain Static from:

Mentioning the subjects' name to a Personality
Divulging any personal information to a Personality
Use of Force against Rosa Dawson
Use of Access to acquire items for personal use
Failure to purchase something while at Clarence Boscow's shop

Triggered events occur any time after the team has reached that level of Static. Control should take into account the presence of any Deep Blue-level Agents involved in the mission and adjust their lists accordingly.

Static levels reset once all Agents eject (or are ejected) from Blue City.

Control should monitor all Static levels during the mission. These levels are classified WHITE-level information and as such are freely available to members of Control.

Agent vs. Agent Rules

"He came at me like a mad dog, screaming about what he saw. I had to take him out."

If two or more player-controlled Agents come into conflict, the following rules are used:

One point of Static is immediately earned per Agent involved in the conflict.

All participating Agents state their intentions and make the appropriate die rolls (using either Force or Instinct) – the results are added to their Heart Rates.

The Agent that rolls highest wins the conflict unless an Agent wishes to escalate the conflict, in which case everyone who wishes to continue rolls again. This generates more Static (one point per Agent rolling again). Agents are free to drop out of (and forfeit) the conflict anytime before the dice are rolled. If the Agents are engaged in life-threatening behavior, the risky action rules should be used (penalties are applied once the conflict is resolved).

This process continues until all the Agents drop out or the conflict stands.

[redacted]

Impaired Access

If an Agent compromises the Company or her fellow Agents, it could provoke an immediate response from Control. The Agent must make an Access roll (Commendation Points may be spent but neither talents nor Techniques may be used). Failure results in temporary loss of one point of Access. If Access ever falls to 0, that Agent is immediately pulled from the mission, labeled a security risk and removed from active duty.

Special Rules for Deep Blue-level Agents

Welcome to the big leagues, Agent. You're one of us now.

Upon promotion to Deep Blue-level clearance, Senior Agents have access to the following new rules:

Team Leader

Senior Agents are always made the Lead Agent at the start of a mission. They're assumed to be in charge of the team, hand out assignments and call for ejection rolls should the junior Agents become impaired. If two Senior Agents are on a mission, the two Agents should decide who assumes the team leader's role.

Reciprocity [redacted]

Under the Rule of Reciprocity, a Senior Agent may spend a Commendation Point to roll a bonus Access die (as if using an Access Talent). If the Senior Agent already has an Access Talent that pertains to the roll, she may roll two bonus dice.

Example: Senior Agent Dresser has the Access (Intelligence) Talent and is requesting information on their target's present location. If she spends a Commendation Point to activate Reciprocity, she may add two bonus dice to her Access roll (one from her Talent, one from Reciprocity).

[redacted]

New Technique: Seniority

Senior Agents may learn the Seniority Talent and use it to reduce Static by 1d6 after spending a Commendation Point. Each additional Commendation Point spent in this manner reduces the Static by another 1d6 points. Seniority may only be taught to other Senior Agents.

Private Static [redacted]

A Senior Agent who reduces the team's Static earns private Static that she must carry for the rest of her career. Whenever a Deep Blue-level Agent spends Commendation Points (for any reason), the Agent earns that many points of private Static.

This number counts as the team's total Static (meaning that the Agent may not lower the team's Static past her own private Static). In the event that multiple Agents possess private Static, only the higher number is counted.

Example: Senior Agent Chessman has 2 private Static while Senior Agent Schaffer has 6. Any team they're both assigned to starts each mission with 6 Static. [redacted]

Special Promotion

[redacted]

What do I want? I want what everyone wants. The question is: are you going to help me?

Blue-level Agents advance in the Company by earning Commendation points. Senior Agents advance by spending them. A Deep Blue-level Agent who spends 10 Commendation Points (and thus earns 10 private Static) is promoted to Black-level security. These Special Agents are never seen or heard from again. They may no longer accompany Blue or Deep Blue-level Agents on missions. [redacted]

Mission debriefings in the past are rife with inaccuracies and conflicting statements but some Agents have reported the following information:

Rogue Black-level Agents are living in Blue City without the Company's knowledge or sanction.

They have no names.

They do not exist.

They answer to no authority…save one.

Awake Asleep

In the last few years, bold experiments in hypnotherapy and neurology have uncovered fantastic secrets. Humans now realize that the last great frontier lies neither beyond our solar system nor underneath the waves. The final frontier lies within us all – in our thoughts, in our dreams and in our memories.

The Nasrudin Institute (a clinic devoted to sleep disorders and dream therapy) discovered the Lacuna purely by accident. Its scientists, researchers and therapists were tasked with the mission to explore our inner spaces and to map the human consciousness. But while pursuing these goals, the members of the Institute uncovered quantifiable proof of a collective unconscious, much like the one proposed by Carl Jung.

Using a complex assortment of techniques (both traditional and esoteric), the walls of the "collective unconscious" were breached by a succession of volunteers. Three subjects were laid out on padded tables and simultaneously brought into R.E.M. sleep. The fourth was placed into a hypnotic state and then put to sleep via intravenous injection. While in this altered state, the hypnotized subject began to describe a strange dream in which he was riding on a bright orange trolley with the other three patients. After fifteen minutes had elapsed, the subjects were awakened and then interviewed by researchers.

What was most curious was that the three dreamers all separately described the same city and the same trolley as the hypnotized subject. Not only that, but they maintained that the hypnotized subject had engaged them in conversation. Subsequent tests validated the subjects' claims. An alternate reality did exist, apart from ours, and could be reached through dreams.

Oceans of Memory

The term "Mnemonic Topography" was coined by the head of research at the Institute. Evidence pointed to several discrete levels of the subconscious. And much like the depths of the ocean hold startlingly different species of life, each mnemonic level carried its own unique "ecosystem." On the "green" or topmost surface, short-term memory and emotions were the waves on the surface of the ocean. Easily seen, they were signifiers of currents and turbulence far below. Memories could be "skimmed" by a trained professional; much like a meteorologist can gauge weather patterns by studying cloud formations.

Down below the surface, the "blue" level seemed to capture the majority of the research team's interest. This unconscious realm of dreams and desires seemed to exist on the periphery of an entire world. One in which the dreams of one person were like dense fogbanks hiding a rocky coastline.

As
mystery
Agents
acting
in
A
NON CORPOREAL
Capacity
Human Frailties
are
NO
LONGER
Areas
of
CONCERN
FOR
The
COMPANY

The Map began to take shape.

Deep within Blue City, places inaccessible to inexperienced travelers, were the levels classified as "deep blue." When some subjects were brought back from parts of deep blue with severe psychological problems, these areas were designated "black" and further exploration was prohibited except in specially monitored sessions. Black-level seemed to have some relation to nightmares and night terrors, an inhospitable environment with (psychically) crushing depths and hostile life forms.

While charting out this dangerous area, a kind of trench was discovered…a fissure running along the "floor" of the mnemonic topography like a rift in the seabed resulting from seismic activity. This seemingly bottomless pit was called the Lacuna.

> ***Lacuna***
> *Literally, a pit. Also, a missing piece or a blank space. A psychic black hole so dense that not even memory can escape its pull.*

When the Map was near-completion, more and more time and resources was spent exploring the Lacuna and the area around it. The Nasrudin Institute was placed under the scrutiny of government agencies and its therapeutic research was farmed out to similar clinics. The Institute now had one purpose and one purpose alone: unlock the secrets of the Lacuna.

Sirius Makes First Contact

Early human experimentation could not be avoided and we have only just begun to learn of these early forays into the Lacuna. Naturally, volunteer subjects were unsuitable (both for technical and for ethical reasons) and convicted felons were used instead.

One of these subjects was a serial rapist and murderer codenamed Sirius. While under hypnosis, Sirius described a cadre of strange beings that followed him through the streets of a vast city. These beings appeared to be humanoid and dressed in some kind of antiquated uniform. A portion of his transcript follows:

[redacted]

SESSION: #112 SUBJECT: #16 ("Sirius")

CONTROLLER: #14-b ("Nader")

SIRIUS: I can't get away from them.

CONTROL: Who? Who is chasing you?

SIRIUS: I told you. I can't see them. They're all shadowed. I can hear them coming.

CONTROL: Can you see anything?

SIRIUS: Uh, yeah. It's dark but I can see a little. I just ducked into an alley. Hiding behind a dumpster. [redacted] It's cold and I think it's snowing or something. Raining. Uh…uh, it's freezing.

CONTROL: And those men? Are they still chasing you?

SIRIUS: I…no. Wait…I hear footsteps.

At this point the subject's heart rate jumps dramatically

SIRIUS: Oooh no. No…no.

CONTROL: What? What do you see?

SIRIUS: I…uh, I have to go. I have to get away…

Subject began to thrash violently

CONTROL: You're okay [redacted]. You're okay. Nothing can hurt you.

SIRIUS: I…don't…I don't think so. I can see them now. I need to go now.

CONTROL: What do you see?

SIRIUS: Oh, god. Oh, god. Spidermen. Spiders. I gotta move. I see a door.

CONTROL: Spiders?

SIRIUS: Spid…I'm [redacted] inside. I see her. I see her with a little boy. [redacted] She's reaching for me…help me…I'm here…

At this point this subject's heart rate returns to normal and he leaves REM sleep. No other contact is made during the session and the subject insists that he remembers nothing when he awakens. Subject appears extraordinarily calm and passive. Asks for a glass of milk.

Further inquiries substantiated the claims of these "spidermen." Humanoid creatures with arachnid-like faces, dressed in some kind of outdated Eastern Bloc-style uniform. These beings appear to be hostile to human interlopers though their origins are a complete mystery. No attempt at communication has proven successful.

The identity of the "girl" from Sirius' final session has yet to be established. Additional investigation has proven the existence of a mysterious female character. She does not appear in further sessions with Sirius but her existence is confirmed by other researchers working with various other subjects.

Sirius himself has since become a model prisoner and professes to remember nothing of his life since his parents died in a fire when he was a child and he was sent to a foster family. This memory loss persists up to and including the first encounter with the unidentified female dream character.

Identity of the "little boy" in session #112 has been established as Sirius at approximately age six. [redacted]

Prisons Without Walls

After the prison experiments concluded, several theories came to light:

// The shared dream-space (now called "Blue City") exists outside and alongside our own reality. It appears to host its own population apart from human personalities engaged in R.E.M.-stage sleep.

// The Lacuna is some kind of mnemonic "black hole" that eats memories and subconscious thought. Although it cannot be explicitly located within Blue City, it is somehow connected with Unidentified Female Dream Character Omega (a.k.a. "The Girl").

// The Spidermen exist in Blue City, perhaps as some kind of autonomous agents (?) or as a kind of psychic projection (much like the City itself appears to be a psychic projection).

// Memory loss and extreme personality shifts follow contact with the Lacuna. Violent criminal offenders appear to be pacified and "cured" of violent psychosexual impulses after contact with the Lacuna, though we don't know why or how this happens.

Years later, some mysteries remain but others have been solved. Using the techniques pioneered by the Nasrudin Institute and developed during the prison experiments, it is now possible to excise a violent personality from its host consciousness. The process is not unlike how a surgeon slices away cancerous tissue from its surroundings.

Prisons are now a thing of the past. It no longer makes sense to lock up an individual when they're not the ones at fault. Humans are basically good people. The hostile personality is what drives them to their ends…it's a sickness. And once the hostile personality (or "HP") is dealt with, the subject is able to be re-integrated into the populace as a functional, compassionate and conscientious member of society. The criminal mind has been revealed as a kind of disease, one with a permanent cure.

Now all that was needed were people to carry out this new initiative.

Origins

Advances in so-called 'dream technologies" have yielded more advanced equipment and protocols, as well as a method of mnemonic alteration using something called the "Lacuna Device."

Lacuna Device
This button-sized device is used to send its wearer to a "metaphysical black hole." The device must be pinned onto the subject and is then activated by twisting it to the right. a three-second delay, the subject is summarily dispatched to the Lacuna. Modern devic are emblazoned with the Mystery Agent logo and can only be used by the agent assign carry that specific device.

A specialized task force had to be created to patrol Blue City for HP's mete out rehabilitation using the Lacuna Device. The Mystery Agents were formed from the core members of the prison experiments. "The Company," along with the police departments, the FBI and other public health agencies, began its war against the disease of violence.

Recent Developments

Because of the overwhelming success of the Lacuna Project, the Company is in the process of expanding its services. Mystery Agents now work with violent offenders of all stripes, not just those accused of the most heinous crimes. Superintendent Pastor's goal of "a better, safer world" is on its way to becoming a reality.

The Creation of the Mystery

The following interview took place on September 17, 2004 with a Mystery Agent who did not wish to be identified. Alterations and edits have been made where appropriate in order to preserve anonymity. Game notes have been inserted as necessary.

"It's not the work, it's the stairs."

"It is unclear whether the Nasrudin Institute created or discovered the Lacuna. One theory is that it was always there, waiting to be discovered. The other theory is that the Institute's experiments split open the collective unconscious like weeds splitting cracks in poured concrete. Of course, up until recently, the collective unconscious was a theory too.

"Still, with the advent of the Mystery Agents, crime has plummeted. And not just violent crime, either. It seems that by working on the diseased parts of society, the entire body has slowly begun to heal. People are happier. Streets are clean and quiet. The world is coming to order at last, and not under the auspices of jackbooted thugs and tanks and police states, either.

What most amazes the general public is how quiet the whole process is.

"A few people lying down in a sealed room, wires and electrodes hooked up to their chests and temples. Racks of shiny medical equipment waiting in the wings. A lot of technical-looking people watching monitors and EKG's, talking constantly and speaking into throat-mikes taped to their necks. Sometimes music (something subtle and relaxing, no Beethoven), sometimes candles or aromatherapy. New Age hokum is mixed with Information Age technology."

Groundwork at Green-level

"There are still police departments in every city. And aside from a rapid downturn in police-related deaths (on both sides of the equation), there's no major difference between the police work of today and the police work of yesterday. The big difference is what happens with a body is found. That's when the Mystery Agents step in.

"When some sick bastard starts raping and killing little girls, or when some nut with a grudge and a rifle starts picking off people from a bell tower, Green-level Agents are called in to investigate. If the police or the feds have done their jobs, they'll have a suspect (or at least some solid leads). Mystery Agents will assist them in apprehending suspects and submit them to a procedure called Cursory Mnemonic Exploration (or C.M.E.)."

Author's Note: Agents are typically briefed on the nature of the mission, given the subject's background and any other pertinent information from a Green-level C.M.E. team. A brief question and answer period is allowed in all but the most time-sensitive cases, then the Agents are sent to the waiting room to prepare for the insertion.

The Slab

"The Slab is our colorful term for the operating theatre where Mystery Agents ply their trade. The subject is sedated and the Exploration Team connects with the subject's mind. From there, the team wanders through Green-level (the 'shallow end' of the mnemonic pool) and pokes around for information regarding the crime (or crimes) being investigated. When evidence is found, it's presented to a review committee of judges, law enforcement personnel, psychiatric experts and at least one Senior Agent. If the evidence is satisfactory, the next phase commences.

"What happens is this: you go to sleep in this world. You wake up someplace else. More specifically, you're locked down into Blue City, a meandering cityscape of the mind. Because it's far too dangerous to just muck around inside someone's head, Blue City acts like a border town that links everyone's heads. And everyone exists inside Blue City. Everyone you've met. People you've never known, people that don't exist.

Once in Blue City, it's best to find out where the other members of the team are. Usually, they'll be close by – within a block or two of wherever you end up. Sometimes, things happen and the distances increase."

Author's Note: Although there is a standard dress uniform, an Agent dresses in loose-fitting comfortable clothing while on a mission: shorts or cotton "pajamas" and bare feet. M.E. personnel use climate control to keep the temperature at optimum levels (sheets are used for privacy purposes as Agents must sleep without much in the way of clothing to allow for heart-rate monitors and the like).

The subject is always prepped in advance so that the Mystery Agents' identities are kept secret. Upon entering the Slab, the Agents are secured, hooked up to various devices and then "dropped" in to Green-level in an unconscious state. After some diagnostics are run, the Agents "wake up" from this state in Blue-level and enter Blue City.

The Lead Agent (aka Team Leader) enters first, with the drop zone determined in advance by M.E. Once the Lead Agent enters and contact is established, the rest of the team follows one by one until all Agents have arrived. It's the team leader's responsibility to search out and locate misplaced team members as soon as possible. Once this is done and all Agents have been accounted for, the Lead Agent calls in to her Monitor to give a status report.

Calling Home

"Getting information or equipment can be done in a few different ways. The easiest way is just to grab a vehicle or whatever once you're inside Blue-level. Control is able to provide just about anything else you'd need that isn't readily available. The trick is to get the request out to them, which can be tricky at times. 'Calling home,' as we call it, involves cutting through the psychic noise separating Control from Blue-level. If you can get to a public payphone or a private phone line, you can dial in requests, which is a lot easier than just sending out a telepathic 'ping' and waiting for the 'pong' to be delivered back to you."

Author's Note: Access rolls must be made to acquire intelligence or equipment while in Blue City. Access may also be used to contact the other Agents (calling someone doesn't necessarily mean that they receive the message…it merely means that the message was successfully sent). Once contact is established, communication may commence (the "call" is effectively over when Control rules the conversation is over or when one of the parties "hangs up").

Equipment can be delivered from Control to the Agents, but it's a tricky process and apt to go awry.

Delivery can take a variety of forms:

- // Agents may find an equipment cache in their general area.
- // Conscripted Personalities can hand-deliver equipment (or tell the Agents where the drop point is located).
- // Equipment (especially small items such as money or weapons) can materialize on the Agent's person. This is usually done by having the item "appear" in the Agent's pocket or when dramatically appropriate – for example, an unarmed Agent facing a Hostile spins around and "draws" a pair of revolvers from within her coat…guns that up to a moment ago did not exist.

Some Techniques allow Agents to enter Blue City with equipment already on their persons.

Blue City

"Blue City is beautiful in the way a sad girl can be beautiful…gray and lonely and lovely. It's always raining and the sun never shines in Blue City. The cold wind whips against the brick and stone walls of a multitude of buildings. Everything seems so much larger and deeper and darker. It's the City writ large, surrounded by cool blue waves. Personalities drift in and out like ghosts. They materialize in the corner of your eye and when you turn to focus in on them, they sharpen like slides under a microscope. Everything comes into detail and every mote of dust is like another world.

"Sometimes I feel like I'm in a dream, which…well, obvious. Other times, it's more…like I've gone backward in time. Everything seems a little archaic. Like the cars look different. And people dress and talk…different. And little things, neon signs, automats…when's the last time you went to an automat? The newspapers are written in some language that looks like Arabic, but isn't. It spins around and blurs out of focus if you try and read it. The food tastes odd. Not bad. Just, more organic…like it was grown in alien soil. I don't really dig it."

Author's Note: One difficulty Agents face is explaining where they are. For all intents and purposes, they are in a fully-functioning alternate reality. It's not a dream world, but it's not the real world. In fact, it is something quite literally in-between the two.

Continued research into Blue City has yielded the following information:

// "Blue City" is not referred to as such by its residents. The population simply refers to it as "The City" without any further explanation. In fact, there appears to be two amorphous areas outside Blue City: "The Country" (an unexplored area which seems to refer to an external sector of Blue City) and an unnamed foreign place only mentioned in reference to "The Conflict."

// The City is divided into several districts named after the tram stations (or more likely, the tram stops are named after the districts). A river cuts Blue City down the approximate center. Canals and plazas further help to divide the city into large blocks. The following district names have been discovered (their locations are not consistent from mission to mission): Abattoir, Boxer, Café, Diamond Square, Factory, Glassworks. Other places of note include: the racetrack (greyhound racing appears to be a popular pastime), the "zoo" (actually a glass-walled conservatory/greenhouse housing exotic and tropical plants), the subway, the café, hotel kiosk at Café Station Plaza and a large crater near Boxer station which is fenced off from closer inspection (rumored to be the site of an attack in the past, perhaps a pre-cursor the Conflict?). Businesses and other buildings appear to be named in an eponymous fashion: the café is called "Café," the hotel is called "Hotel."

// It's assumed the Blue City is at war (or rather, the government controlling Blue City is at war) with a foreign power. This war is called "The War" or "The Conflict" by residents of Blue City. It was first believed that the Spidermen were the enemies in the conflict but research into this area by Alpha ruled this out as impossible. The residents do not seem to be aware of the presence of Hostiles (HP's and Spidermen).

// Popular culture does not seem to exist here, possibly owing to the skewed age demographics. Blue City has street musicians, festivals and concerts but aside from the radio and a primitive movie house, there is no real recorded media. Newspapers and magazines seem to be popular forms of entertainment, as are gambling, playing board games (chess, checkers and regional variations on real-world games) and walking around more scenic areas of the city (despite many reports, the city itself is quite elegant and beautiful in places, with intricate architectural detailing on some of the buildings, elaborate gardens and old-fashioned ironwork in the railings, streetlamps and other details).

// Travel is limited to streetcars, automobiles, bicycles and the like. No air traffic has ever been observed. Foot traffic and public transportation appear to be the leading forms of travel. Trains "to the country" exist but these areas outside Blue City are limited to Agents of Deep-Blue clearance. There is a single industrial district ("Factory") that employs many of the city's adult male populace. Small businesses dominate the streets in the more developed areas and residential areas are the least traveled. It is unclear whether these many apartments and houses are actually populated.

Anomalous incidents that may be anticipated are:

- Skewed perception, especially with regard to alpha-numeric characters
- Sudden shifts in space or time, usually minor
- Personalities appearing in several places (or times) at once
- Personalities appear as other characters (without knowledge of their duplicates)
- Surreal, inexplicable events (contact Mythography for assistance)

Personalities

"There are three types of beings you'll encounter in Blue City. The first are other Mystery Agents. This is the reason for the uniform: quick and easy identification. Blue City is fairly large…larger than any existing metropolitan area. It is possible to run into other Agents on other missions but it doesn't happen too frequently. For the most part, you're on your own."

'Personalities are the second. The P's' are a kind of 'dream character' that appear as random faces in the crowds of Blue City: cab drivers, call girls, bartenders and traffic cops… families walking down the street. Dogs, cats, birds…everything is hyper-realistic but gives off a weird 'vibe' that nobody can pin down. The interesting thing about the P's is they don't realize that they're characters inside a dream. This is why subtlety and discretion are the keystones of the Mystery Agents organization.

"I've met some P's over and over again. Sometimes, they start to remember you, which is nice. It's nice to know people, to have friends outside the Company. This one guy…huge, fat guy wears this crazy straw hat. He sells papers (that I can't read) and food (that I don't eat) from a little cart. His name is Clarence Boscow. Rhymes with 'Boss Cow.' Funny guy."

Hostile Personalities

"Hostile Personalities are just that: personalities, but twisted and wrong. Like cancer feeds off blood in the body HP's consume the flesh of the living in our world, the Real World. To excise the cancer, someone has got to go in and cut it out. Rookie agents have plenty of training about the nature of HP's. How they're emotionless, ruthless, brutal monsters. How they're inhuman in the very real sense of the word. But nothing…nothing can prepare an agent for their first encounter with one of these beasts.

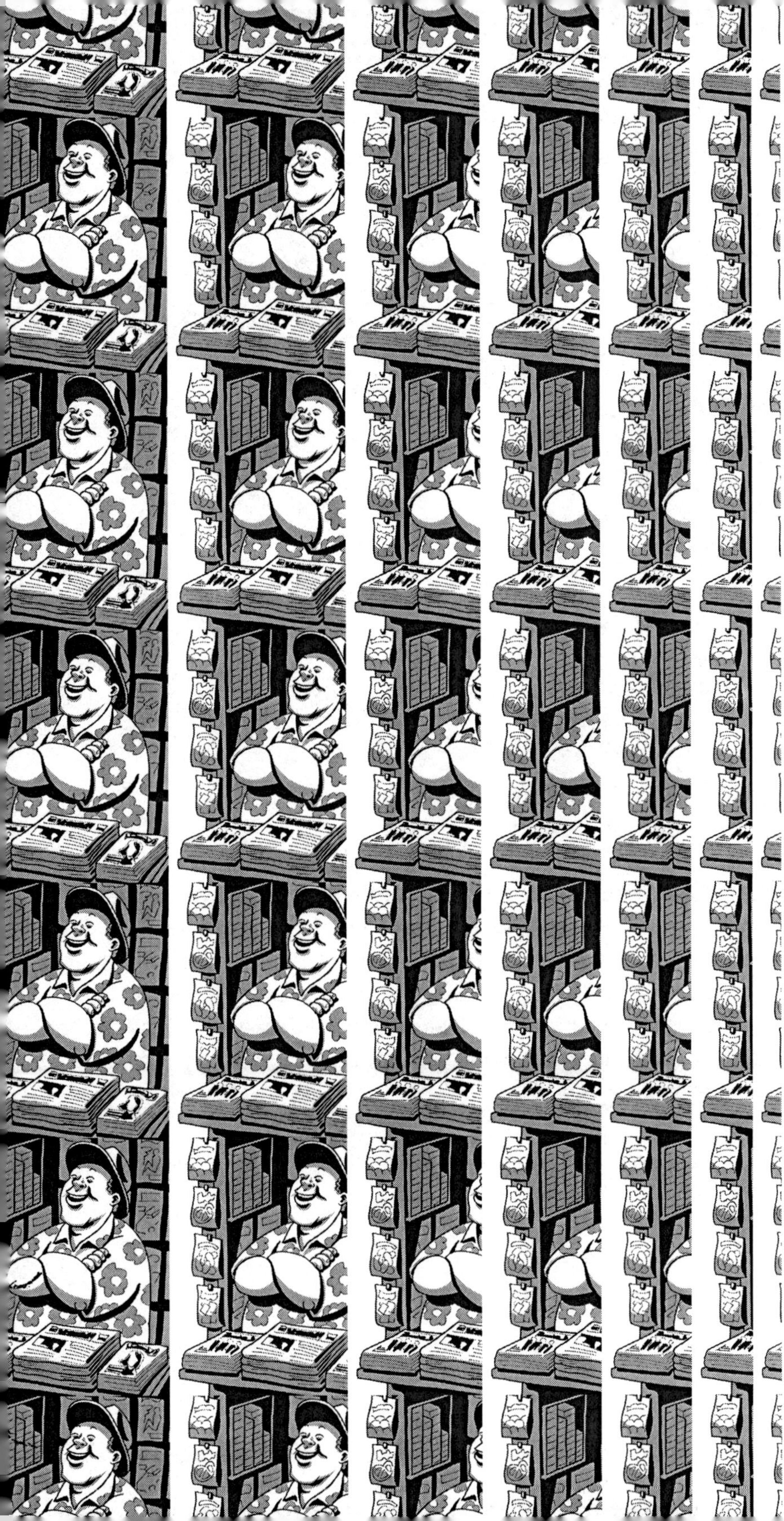

"On the outside, HP's look like their host personalities (the subject of the investigation – the guy or gal laying on the Slab). When it sheds this host body, its true nature is revealed…and it can be a doozy. Fanged mouths surrounded by barbed tentacles, nine-foot tall shaggy black things with too many eyes and too many teeth, reptilian creatures with sinister smiles and poisonous intent. Nothing is too odd, too ugly or too extreme. You can rest assured that as a Mystery Agent, you'll see too much and still never see it all.

"Which brings me to this…"

Spidermen

"The Company, the Institute…hell, just about everyone has questions about the Lacuna and Blue City. These uncharted realms are more mysterious than deep space and we know so little about it all. One of those many mysteries revolves around the Spidermen.

"Rumors about the Spidermen have existed for a while now, ever since the first experiments at the Nasrudin Institute. Sirius and his friends proved that they're not just shadows in the mind. They're real…really real. And if you ever meet one (and you don't just wake up screaming right then and there), you have a whole lot of trouble on your hands."

Author's Note: The creatures usually keep to the sidelines but prolonged contact in Blue City, obvious Mystery Agent activity or just sheer dumb luck can draw them out like dogs hunting down a gob of bloody hamburger.

"No shit, I ran into the Spidermen once. And I didn't wake up screaming. They wanted to know who (the team) was and why we where there. They had weapons, strange little handguns, and demanded identification documents. One of the rookie agents freaked out and opened fire. They pulped him with those weird little guns and took off after us. The mission ended with the rest of us ejecting. The subject and the other agent both died on the Slab. The techs still don't know why."

The Girl from Blue City

"I've never seen her. I don't know anyone who has (or if they have, they haven't told me about it. I don't know anything about it.

"Okay, interview over."

At this point the Mystery Agent grabs a donut from the box on the desk, stands up and walks out of the room. The author is escorted outside and led off the premises where a car is waiting.

The author enters and is driven back through the entrance gates to the Company's grounds. The driver says something in Russian and looks up at the author in the rear-view mirror.

The author looks up from his notes and sees six glistening black eyes staring back.

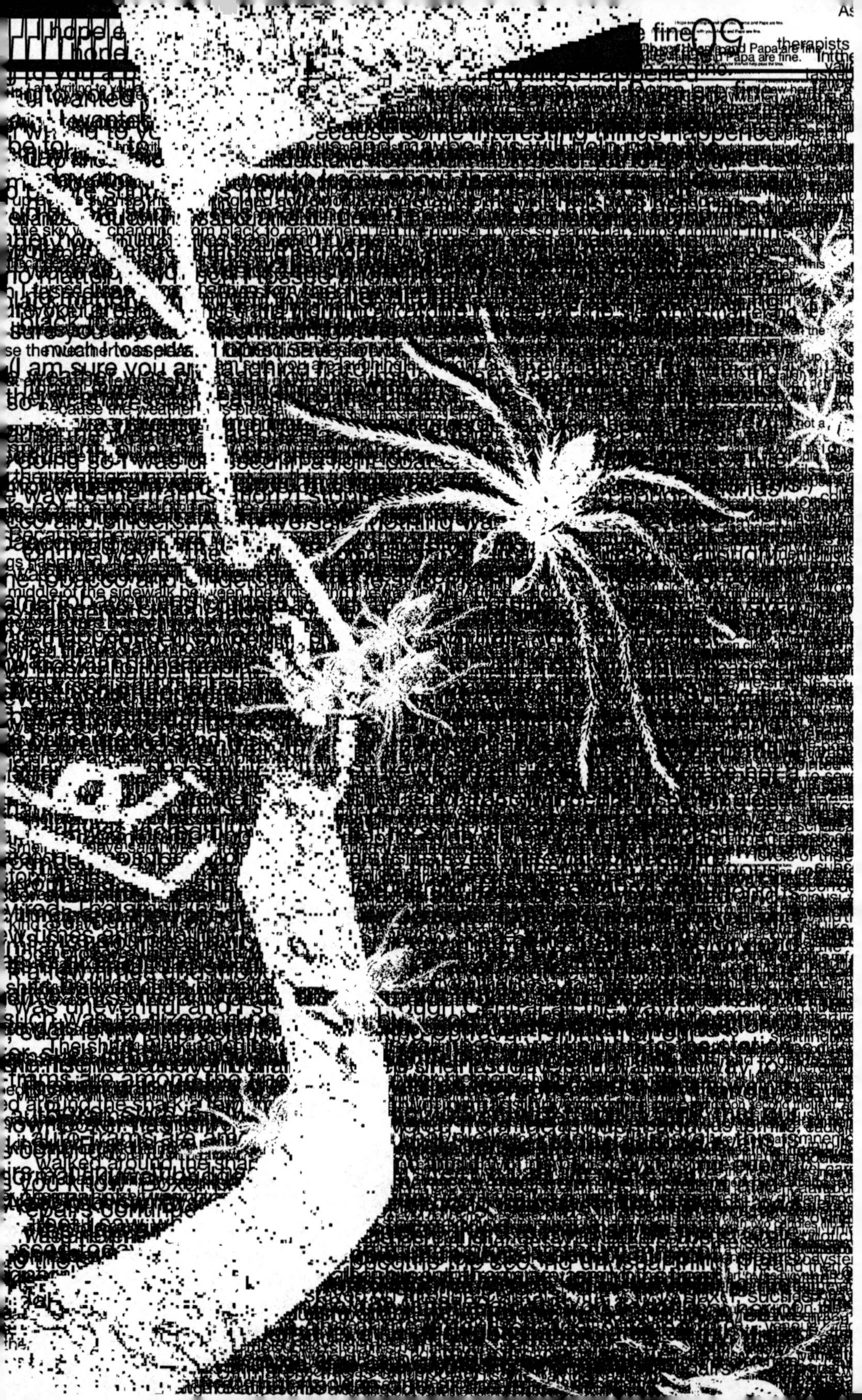

therapists
Papa are fine.
because some interesting things happened
the sky was changing from black to gray when I left the house. It was so early that almost nothing
I am sure you ar
middle of the sidewalk between the

therapists

I hope everything is well with you. Mama and Papa are fine.

I hope everything is well with you.

m writing to you a bit early because some interesting things happened

today and I wanted you to know about them. I understand how hard it

must be for you to be away from us and maybe this will help pass the

wanted you to know about them. I understand how hard it must be for you to be away

black to gray when I left the house. It was so early that almost nothing was open save for the newspaper

woke up before sunrise this morning and could not get back to sleep

no matter how much I tossed and turned.

much I tossed

was open save for the

(I am sure you are laughing hard right now at the image of me waking

Because the weather was pleasant for this time of year

cause the weather was pleasant

is not important to the story but

On the way to the tram station, I stopped in at the kiosk and

Because the weather was pleasant for this time of year

On the way to the tram station, I stopped in at the kiosk and bought

the tobacco and cinders. As I have said,

the cafe -- so I was content to walk to the next stop

Two things happened then

lying in the middle of the sidewalk between the kiosk and the tram stop. At first I thought

not a sculpture but a great fish. The smell is what convinced me. Upon closer

On the way to the tram station (I stopped in at the kiosk and bought some tobacco

Two things happened then

tween the kiosk and the tram stop. At first I thought it to be some kind of

strange street sculpture

As you know, Boxer has still not totally

examination of the thing I saw that it was a large shark, possibly

I noticed something lying in the middle of the sidewalk

smell (as I have said) was terrific. I walked around the shark a few times

The shark was incredibly wide, as if it recently enjoyed a gluttonous

meal, perhaps incredibly wide, as if it recently enjoyed a gluttonous

surrounded by floating, wrinkled white skin. Its gills were dry and

similarly red. The smell (as I have said) was terrific. I walked around the

(such was its size and peculiarity) but I soon

The ride was uneventful and I stayed on through Central all the way to

Boxer, such is my appreciation for this kind of travel. I think that our

auto-trams are among the finest I have ever ridden. Ultimately, this is

walked around the shark a few times

s you know, Boxer has still not totally recovered from the incident and

repairs continue, thus I had to get to the street

om the normal skyway

to the street I saw what would become the second unusual thing

witnessed today: a man, swarthy and mustachioed in the manner of

I assumed

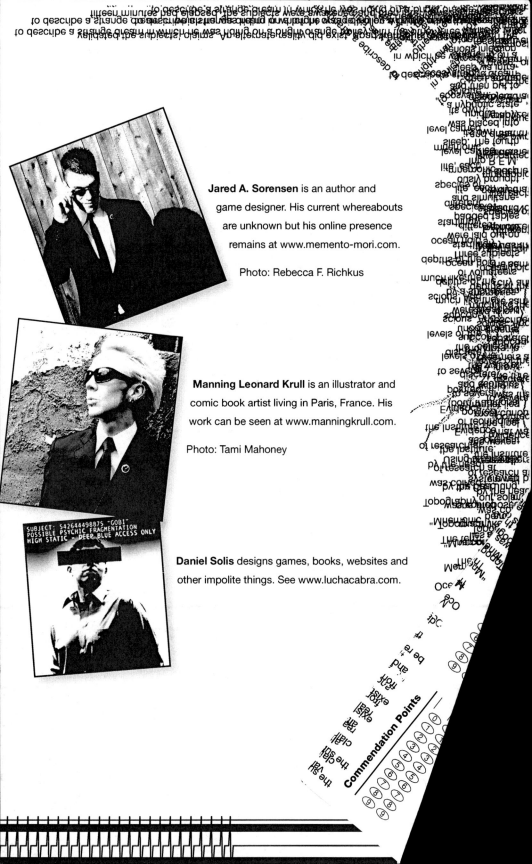

Jared A. Sorensen is an author and game designer. His current whereabouts are unknown but his online presence remains at www.memento-mori.com.

Photo: Rebecca F. Richkus

Manning Leonard Krull is an illustrator and comic book artist living in Paris, France. His work can be seen at www.manningkrull.com.

Photo: Tami Mahoney

Daniel Solis designs games, books, websites and other impolite things. See www.luchacabra.com.

Agent Record Sheet

Pseudonym

A	A	A	A	A	A	A	A	A	A	A	A	A
B	B	B	B	B	B	B	B	B	B	B	B	B
C	C	C	C	C	C	C	C	C	C	C	C	C
D	D	D	D	D	D	D	D	D	D	D	D	D
E	E	E	E	E	E	E	E	E	E	E	E	E
F	F	F	F	F	F	F	F	F	F	F	F	F
G	G	G	G	G	G	G	G	G	G	G	G	G
H	H	H	H	H	H	H	H	H	H	H	H	H
I	I	I	I	I	I	I	I	I	I	I	I	I
J	J	J	J	J	J	J	J	J	J	J	J	J
K	K	K	K	K	K	K	K	K	K	K	K	K
L	L	L	L	L	L	L	L	L	L	L	L	L
M	M	M	M	M	M	M	M	M	M	M	M	M
N	N	N	N	N	N	N	N	N	N	N	N	N
O	O	O	O	O	O	O	O	O	O	O	O	O
P	P	P	P	P	P	P	P	P	P	P	P	P
Q	Q	Q	Q	Q	Q	Q	Q	Q	Q	Q	Q	Q
R	R	R	R	R	R	R	R	R	R	R	R	R
S	S	S	S	S	S	S	S	S	S	S	S	S
T	T	T	T	T	T	T	T	T	T	T	T	T
U	U	U	U	U	U	U	U	U	U	U	U	U
V	V	V	V	V	V	V	V	V	V	V	V	V
W	W	W	W	W	W	W	W	W	W	W	W	W
X	X	X	X	X	X	X	X	X	X	X	X	X
Y	Y	Y	Y	Y	Y	Y	Y	Y	Y	Y	Y	Y
Z	Z	Z	Z	Z	Z	Z	Z	Z	Z	Z	Z	Z

Security Clearance

- ◯ Green
- ◯ Deep Blue
- ◯ Blue
- ◯ Black

Attributes

Force ⓪ ① ② ③ ④

- ◯ Aggression
- ◯ Athletics
- ◯ Strategy

Instinct ⓪ ① ② ③ ④

- ◯ Investigation
- ◯ Communication
- ◯ Intuition

Access ⓪ ① ② ③ ④

- ◯ Logistics
- ◯ Intelligence
- ◯ Navigation

Techniques

Standard Tree

- Achievement Ⓨ Ⓝ
- Endurance Ⓨ Ⓝ
- Meditation Ⓨ Ⓝ
- Training Ⓨ Ⓝ

Assets Tree Ⓨ Ⓝ

- Armed Ⓨ Ⓝ
- Bulletproof Ⓨ Ⓝ
- Caller Ⓨ Ⓝ
- Driver Ⓨ Ⓝ
- ESP Ⓨ Ⓝ

Skills Tree Ⓨ Ⓝ

- Doctor Ⓨ Ⓝ
- Judge Ⓨ Ⓝ
- Spy Ⓨ Ⓝ
- Thief Ⓨ Ⓝ
- Writer Ⓨ Ⓝ

Cover Tree Ⓨ Ⓝ

- Contact Ⓨ Ⓝ
- Credit Ⓨ Ⓝ
- Documents Ⓨ Ⓝ
- Identity Ⓨ Ⓝ
- Safe-House Ⓨ Ⓝ

Restricted Ⓨ Ⓝ

- Seniority Ⓨ Ⓝ

Mentor

- ◯ Agent Gardiner
- ◯ Senior Instructor Snyder
- ◯ Senior Agent Chambers
- ◯ Senior Agent Baxter
- ◯ Special Agent Miner
- ◯ Agent Duke
- ◯ Chief Agent Wagner
- ◯ Vice-Director Forester

Medical History

Gender Ⓜ Ⓕ

Age		Resting Heart Rate			Target Heart Rate			—			Maximum Heart Rate		
0	0	0	0	0	0	0	0	0	0	0	0	0	0
1	1	1	1	1	1	1	1	1	1	1	1	1	1
2	2	2	2	2	2	2	2	2	2	2	2	2	2
3	3	3	3	3	3	3	3	3	3	3	3	3	3
4	4	4	4	4	4	4	4	4	4	4	4	4	4
5	5	5	5	5	5	5	5	5	5	5	5	5	5
	6	6	6	6	6	6	6	6	6	6	6	6	6
	7	7	7	7	7	7	7	7	7	7	7	7	7
	8	8	8	8	8	8	8	8	8	8	8	8	8
	9	9	9	9	9	9	9	9	9	9	9	9	9

Private Static	
0	0
1	1
2	2
3	3
4	4
5	5
6	6
7	7
8	8
9	9

CPSIA information can be obtained at www.ICGtesting.com
Printed in the USA
BVOW082234120812

297702BV00003B/7/P